THE TALE OF HARRY HA

To Freddie & Lily

Happy Halloween

BY CHRIS WADDINGTON

ISBN 978-1-78808-781-0

Dedicated to Nevaeh, My beautiful Grandaughter

This is a story about a weird lad

Called Harry Halloween

If you ever saw him

You'd know what I mean

He is a little strange

It has to be said

Harry has a big pumpkin for a head!

Harry lives in a spooky castle

At the top of a hill

With a couple of friendly ghosts

Called Bernie and Bill

Not a fan of the light

Harry sleeps all day

Only coming out at night

What is Harry's favourite day of the year?

I bet you can guess

Here's a clue

Trick or treat and fancy dress

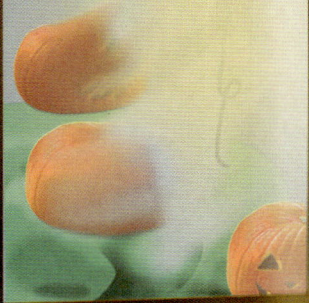

Some people think it is cursed

But Harry can't wait for October the 31st

He doesn't need to worry about an outfit

For the big day

Just look at his wacky wardrobe

He always dresses that way!

Finally its here!!

Each and every Halloween

Harry's place is quite the scene

Witches brewing up potions

Wizards casting the odd spell

Black cats flying on broomsticks

Not to mention a ghost train as well

Early evening

Harry and his mates take to the street

To enjoy a little trick or treat

Then it's back to the castle

To celebrate

With a huge party that's simply great

A magical night

Full of screams and scares

Apple dunking

Musical chairs

Lots of fiendish food to munch

And a cauldron full of boiling punch

Then at midnight

The castle grounds are set alight

Fireworks decorate the sky

As another Halloween passes by

The next day

All the guests are gone

But..

Harry parties on

He is driving Bernie & Bill round the bend

But Harry doesn't want Halloween to end

For Harry Halloween

You can keep Christmas and New Year

He prefers a day filled with frights and fear

Forget the spring and summer too

They leave Harry feeling blue

For this freaky lad

There's only one thing

That makes his heart sing…….

HALLO

HALLO

WEEN